BROKEN

Volume 1

Ian D. Erickson

Library of Congress Cataloging-in-Publication Data:
Ian D. Erickson
Broken, vol 1 / Ian D. Erickson
ISBN: 978-0-6151-9252-9 (pbk)

LCCN: 2008923302

For information about permission to reproduce selections from this book, email Stephanie Freeland [image_marketing_co@yahoo.com].

Manufactured in the United States of America by
www.Lulu.com – Online Publisher

Book design/layout by Stephanie Freeland & Dr. Beverly G. Busch
Cover/interior art/photography by Stephanie Freeland
Editing by Dr. Beverly G. Busch

Set in 1942 Report & Arial

CONTACT

author:
ianderickson@gmail.com

booking:
image_marketing_co@yahoo.com

For Lance Corporal (USMC)

Philip E. Frank

BROKEN

TABLE OF CONTENTS

Foreword

Bold. Raw. Real . . .

When a new writer bursts onto the literary scene, the heavens open, and when a Christian writer emerges, the planets take notice. And make no mistake: Ian D. Erickson is not just another writer of pretty Christian verse. Rather, he is a Christian poet in the finest Christian literary tradition. His is a Christian message of love and redemption couched in broken humanity. Erickson's voice mingles strident argument with unapologetic longing, suspends it in tight poetic form, and overlays it all with a 21st c. jagged edge. His expression spans the pain and strain of a completely shattered and fractured modern world. His poems speak of humanity at its darkest hour. He speaks of love lost, betrayal, personal struggle, toxic relationships, and false messiahs. His poems, in fact, portray Christ, and Him crucified. But this is no churchy, pseudo-religious expression. Far from it! Rather, we see Him broken and beaten, crucified and left to die in every tortured scene Erickson portrays. And yet, through it all, through the brokenness and pain, Erickson points the way to the **Truth** available to us all, if we had but eyes to see and ears to hear.

January 22, 2007
Dr. Beverly G. Busch

And ye shall know the truth, and the truth shall make you free.

Jhn 8:32 KJV

Preface

As a young boy, I was always fascinated with the idea of God. Being raised a Catholic, I was introduced to Him at a young age. I can remember going to church every Sunday morning. I was excited. My parents thought I was nuts. They had never seen a boy who couldn't wait to go to church. My grandfather on my mother's side always told his friends I would make the family proud by becoming a priest. I did want to make them proud. As I grew older and ideas of church and God began to fade, I found out the only reason my parents went to church was so to get supermarket gift certificates that my grandmother would give them. They never cared about God or Jesus. They just wanted money.

Through this time my home life deteriorated. I remember many nights crying out to God to take me out of this hell. I then became very angry with God when I was fifteen. That is when my parents divorced. I could not handle it anymore. I was then His enemy and hated Him. I once loved Him but now I could not stand Him. I began to dress in all black and listened to "devil worshiping music." I wanted to get as far away from God as I could. I began to hurt myself and ended up being institutionalized for suicide attempts. They then loaded me up on heavy sedatives. I was so confused and scared. One thing I did know was I hated God.

I was diagnosed Bi Polar, a label I still carry to this day. As time went on I began to drink and use drugs. I engaged in high risk behaviors such as heavy drug use and unprotected sex. I did not care about living. I hated it and these behaviors were the only way I knew how to cope. I sang in many rock bands and this only helped to push me further into the gutter. I continued to self mutilate and practiced witchcraft. I wanted to be in control of things. I liked the feeling of being able to have say over a particular outcome. It's ironic. Something I thought I had control over was so absolutely out of control.

At the age of 22 I began to search more. My life was wearing me out and if I carried on like this I would die. I was close to death many times in this period from overdosing, suicide attempts, and becoming ill as a result of running my body into the ground. It had to end so I turned to a familiar book, the Bible. I tore through it and wanted to believe it. The only problem was I did not believe all of it. Now, if I could not believe all of it then I could believe none of it. A close friend of mine was recently saved and introduced me to apologetics (defense of the faith). As time went on and read more I realized I could trust the Word of God. In August of 2003 I surrendered my life to Christ. Ever since then my real purpose began. I was the reacquainted with an old friend.

I have always been a writer. I have been writing stories and even poetry since I was 5. It has always been a passion of mine and one that I could not live without. Writing, especially the writing of poetry, helps me organize my thoughts. The whole process is very sacred to me. It allows me to understand my inner turmoil and then transfer this understanding to paper. I do not quite understand the processes myself. It is as if my hand simply dances in time to the tune of my mind. Somebody recently asked me what inspires me. I was confounded when I couldn't come up with an answer right away. I was expecting to say something like "God" but that wasn't completely it. Yes, God is my inspiration, but it would have not answered the question appropriately. What I responded with was, "I do not get inspired because I am in a constant state of inspiration." My reason is that I can set myself in and write about any subject at anytime. It is as if my mind has a switch that is stuck in the "on" position. I am not quite sure what it is, but what I do know is that God has everything to do with it.

Also as a writer there is a sort of altruistic nature that goes along with me being able to express how I feel. I am able to release the thoughts running around madly in my head and place them onto paper. It is my hope that readers can also relate to what I am saying and apply that to their lives. This is the point of my book.

It is not called *Broken* because I thought it was simply a catchy title. When I say I am broken, I mean it in the context of being hurt and feeling pain. Now since I feel these things, because I am broken, I look for my solution or sedative to numb these common reactions to a world that is fractured and fragmented. Where I look is really the theme. Did I look to drugs? Yes. Did I look to alcohol? Yes. Did I look to sex? Yes. Were any of these things able to fix the brokenness and make my situation less painful? NO! I was stuck in a cycle. I would become hurt. I would engage in one of the above listed behaviors and as a result become hurt even more. As a result of being hurt even more, I would engage in more. I would simply consume more. As a result of that I would become more hurt and the cycle went on and on and on.

Now, if things of this world could not be the solution, what was? My poetry and writings give an answer to that question. Christ. He, whose body was broken for me, broke the bondage, and fixed my broken spirit. So the theme of brokenness is not only within us and my writing but in God Himself. He was also broken. He was shamed, abused and beaten. He took on my brokenness. That is why He came. It is through His brokenness, through His crucifixion and resurrection, that I am made whole.

All the pieces in this book have been written after I believed in Christ. It shows the struggles I go through even though I do have a foundation to turn to. I am not perfect; I still struggle with sin. Nevertheless, through the bleakness of this world I have somebody to rest in and turn to for help. It is no longer sex, drugs and rock and roll, but God Himself. He is the truth, the way and the life. When I do stumble I know HE will receive me with open arms and wipe away my tears. I know He will carry me through hard times. And I know I will meet Him in **Eternity** one day.

Broken could not be as perfectly put together without the help of Dr. Beverly G. Busch, Head of General Education Department at Somerset Christian College. Her time, effort, and energy were the dynamic behind this work.

Ian D. Erickson

Man at his worst

Fragmented.

Fractured.

Reflecting.

Darkness.

Sin.

God at His Best

Salvation.

Crucifixion.

Enter.

Eternity.

Psalm 38

ודמע קחרמ יבורק
"My neighbors stay far away…"

[1] [[A Psalm of David, to bring to remembrance.]] O LORD, rebuke me not in thy wrath: neither chasten me in thy hot displeasure. [2] For thine arrows stick fast in me, and thy hand presseth me sore. [3] [There is] no soundness in my flesh because of thine anger; neither [is there any] rest in my bones because of my sin. [4] For mine iniquities are gone over mine head: as an heavy burden they are too heavy for me. [5] My wounds stink [and] are corrupt because of my foolishness. [6] I am troubled; I am bowed down greatly; I go mourning all the day long. [7] For my loins are filled with a loathsome [disease]: and [there is] no soundness in my flesh. [8] I am feeble and sore broken: I have roared by reason of the disquietness of my heart. [9] Lord, all my desire [is] before thee; and my groaning is not hid from thee. [10] My heart panteth, my strength faileth me: as for the light of mine eyes, it also is gone from me. [11] My lovers and my friends stand aloof from my sore; and my kinsmen stand afar off. [12] They also that seek after my life lay snares [for me]: and they that seek my hurt speak mischievous things, and imagine deceits all the day long. [13] But I, as a deaf [man], heard not; and [I was] as a dumb man [that] openeth not his mouth. [14] Thus I was as a man that heareth not, and in whose mouth [are] no reproofs. [15] For in thee, O LORD, do I hope: thou wilt hear, O Lord my God. [16] For I said, [Hear me], lest [otherwise] they should rejoice over me: when my foot slippeth, they magnify [themselves] against me. [17] For I [am] ready to halt, and my sorrow [is] continually before me. [18] For I will declare mine iniquity; I will be sorry for my sin. [19] But mine enemies [are] lively, [and] they are strong: and they that hate me wrongfully are multiplied. [20] They also that render evil for good are mine adversaries; because I follow [the thing that] good [is]. [21] Forsake me not, O LORD: O my God, be not far from me. [22] Make haste to help me, O Lord my salvation.

Psa 38:1-22 KJV

Declaring the end
from the beginning,
and from ancient
times the things
that are not yet
done, saying, my
counsel shall stand,
and I will do all my
pleasure. Isa 46:10 KJV

It Was Going to End

(Heartache is the greatest Muse of all . . .)

Respectfully yet vividly
Sadly and anxiously
Intrinsically and eventually
    It was going to end.

Know this. Ones that share in this mentality
Can't find compatibility.
Welcome to the experience!
    It was going to end.

And with all our ability
That all aspects have a mortality
As I awaited tentatively
    It was going to end.

What had a semblance of stability
That warped reality
Attends to infrequently
    It was going to end.

So I raise my absent credibility
There is no room for feasibility
Only God dictates Eternity
    It was going to end.

Separation Anxiety

What can one assume when all we do is consume?

To break the parade just to make the grade

 Would be a miserable endeavor,

And it's back to forever, forever falling like Satan's angels.

So hands once clasped never did last in a bleak existence.

All I can do is forget forever and continue on in my loathsome

persistence.

Frigid weather overtakes my soul like the void of a black hole.

And who can control all that we hold in a world of a putrid

atmosphere?

I am slowly turning to stone as if Medusa has got a hold

On my heart, turning even the maggots away.

What a horrible man I am when I cannot even preach what I practice!

The needs of myself have surpassed all expectations of my own

relations,

And to die tonight would be oh! so blissful! if it were not so sinful.

The woman saith unto him, I know that Messiah cometh, which is called Christ: when he is come, he will tell us all things. Jhn 4:25 KJV

A Penny-less Thank You

(I have no money, so happy birthday!)

When the world wobbles wickedly and the tears flow,

When the earth evaporates endlessly and the fears grow,

When the life I survive selects an end,

When the bottle slipped and fell from my hand,

A smile as bright as a light shining through the night appeared.

A voice so soothing, saturating and celebrating my existence,

Arms outstretched like a descending angel's wings,

Arriving with words of wisdom from His well spring,

My heart's desire was met by you.

You wipe away my tears and tell me it's all untrue.

My self immolation you cannot stand.

I have yet to comprehend or even understand.

You say it's "God's will" and your mission is I.

Thoughts of such compassion press tears against my eyes.

This devotion to me is uncanny and unnecessary!

This promotion of me is undeserved and unwarranted!

My Gaelic angel who stands in the gap, like a lighthouse leading ships ashore,

How can one continue to care about a recalcitrant rebel?

How can one continue to stare at a man so un- level?

You give joy when the darkness divides.

You bring motherly affection when the tides rise.

If my heart were not as black as coal, I would thank you from the bottom of it.

So I will praise you for retrieving my soul from a burning, bottomless pit.

Thank you for the warmth and listening to my pleas.

Taking away anxieties, it means so much to me.

I suppose in the meantime I will be a brat,

One only a mother can love. And I thank you for that.

A Glimpse of Heaven

A woman clothed in virtue

Would certainly explode!

A woman that would subdue

All that I've been sold!

To warm the ancient chill of my bones at night,

Her fingers caress.

To fade away evil's will of a heart contrite,

Softly she speaks of selflessness.

A woman of virtue finer than gold,

A treasure more valuable than Alexandria's lost tomes.

A woman of virtue, heir to behold

A long- past memory that has become shown.

Does this heavenly dove exist?

Or is she a fabrication?

Will she be my exorcist?

Can I find her within this eon?

A love that is more than love,

A respect that considers God above,

A mystical muse that would not just amuse.

Oh, to be wrapped restful in the arms of such one,

Yes, with eyes brighter than even than the sun!

Where are you my metaphorical mystery?

How much longer must I be alone in my misery?

Ah, a woman of virtue is calling my name,

A woman of virtue, the opposite of all things profane.

A woman of virtue with the skin of an angel!

Yes! A love that would last and not need a sequel!

Close to Corpus Christi

She bends her body, boundless and beautiful.

She twists her entrancing arms erotically.

Erotic, her hips sway as if an alluring aphrodisiac.

Blinding my brain, she is benevolent and bountiful.

She engages electric elements enigmatically.

Her mystical movements become my amorous attack.

Lead me into your temple of treasures so taste full.

Alas, your fine frame erratically eludes.

Your tender stare has become my Prozac.

Wickedly wrapping, wondrous when wrathful,

You do these things because you are emotionally,

Effortlessly, in love with a dream of a necrophiliac.

How hard is it to allow me in

When my love continues to love all your contrived guilt and sin?

Light in the Darkness

You bring solace to a sapped society.

You bring fluttering eyelids to the erratic.

Yes, globe of reflection, you are night's key.

You erase all memories of the day's static.

You bring with you a mystique driven into humanity.

You bring a collective consciousness of the unknown.

Yet, your gentle glow can bring about insanity.

Even His Son was arrested under you; even He was prone.

The pagans gather to collect your energy;

The heathens rather recollect stories of self pity.

The dead souls roam the earth, restless and foreboding.

The dead souls groan from hurt,

Tactless and never leaving,

Tales of vicious creatures lurking behind a corner,

Licking their lips at the thought of tasting man's blood,

They creep quietly, creating cataclysmic cords within us.

They are thoughts of humanity and of course these we cannot trust.

Oh, great moon so pale and bright!

Oh, great moon, that brings light to the night!

Is it a wonder that you are such an ominous figure?

You give the only light and allow our eyes a fight.

You were crafted carefully by the Creator Himself.

How did we come to define you as something else?

You mirror the soul of every godly person,

A penetrating light in a world full of darkness.

You reflect God's heavenly lesson!

In a filthy sea of insecurity, you are truly blessed!

A Man Enjoys His Life:

A Very Short Story

He shifts quickly to his seat as he gently waves to the bartender. "A pint of Smithwicks, please," he says as the female barmaid receives him with a warm smile, her lips quickly sliding over her white teeth. His eyes scan the multitude of TVs over the bar when the barmaid puts down a napkin and gingerly places his pint upon it.

And now he is just an observer of his surroundings. Still feeling lonely in a semi crowded pub, he thinks to himself that this pint will make it crowded, yet he is still lonely. He watches the two bartenders, moving back and forth, opening up bottles, dropping pints and pouring shots, attend to the patrons.

Smoke and laughter fill the scenery like a thunderstorm rolling into a silent summer night. He wonders what his purpose, his goal is. And why would he ponder such thoughts in a jovial place such as this? As he delves deeper into the recesses of his mind, the conclusion slips out of his hands like the land of a mighty tyrant once in power. So what is this conclusion he wonders. Is it slavery to the drink? Is it bondage to the cigarettes? Is it the awkward glances given to women of allure? Those cannot be the answers he sought out for. Not tonight.

"Another pint, Love," he proclaims pointing to the empty glass. She just nods and pours him another pint. Of all places to find an answer to his inquiries, does he really think he will find it here? That would be absurd in a rational man's universe. But this man, the one throwing down alcoholic beverages, may believe it so. The jukebox blares out all the voices now. It doesn't matter though. They all sound the same in all these venues. Loud screams turn into whispers over engulfing nonsense.

He was enjoying his pint when a man named Paul decided to engage him in conversation. So he stayed talking to Paul about nothing and Kids in the Hall, a Canadian TV show. By this time he had lost track of the pints being placed in front of him. Not that it really mattered. And why should it?

"What do you think?" Paul asked through a drunken smile and glazed over eyes.

He wasn't paying attention but, instead of letting Paul know that he wasn't paying attention and that he hated Paul's company, he simply nodded his head and uttered "ok . . . ." Paul just laughed and slapped his back. The man then felt annoyance well up in him like a fire consuming the wood in a funeral pyre. He hated it when strangers touched him like this. But he laughed along. Paul was absolutely clueless about his true thoughts.

"Last Call!" yelled the barmaid as she bent over the sink to clean some glasses. As she did, the back of her shirt lifted up and an elaborately colored tattoo showed on the small of her back.

"Can you drive me home?" Paul asked. The man's face went blank. "It's only five minutes away. It won't take you that long," Paul explained in hope.

"I can't. I need sleep," replied the man in further agitation. *First he slaps my back as if he were an old friend and now he wants me to drive him home? Is this what Paul does? Not only that, but Paul took a cigarette from me*, the man thought.

"Oh come on, it's really not that long a ride," Paul continued to petition. At this point the man would like to place Paul's teeth into the back of his neck with his fist.

"Really, I can't. I have to sleep," he retorted, this time more seriously. He turned his head and the male bartender gave him his tab. He placed his credit card on top of it. The male bartender took it promptly over to the cash register. Out of the corner of his eye he could see his new 'best friend' uttering something under his breath as he pushed himself out of the barstool. The bartender came up to him with the total. He signed it and left a tip.

"Alright guys, have a good night," the bartender said with a smile. At this time the man's new pal was gone. *Must be in the bathroom*, the man thought. He walked out to his car. It was dark. Not just outside but inside. He put his key in the lock, turned it and then …

THE END

24

I Am So Amazing to Everybody but Myself

To be alone by the pale moon light

It is always such a fright!

Loneliness causes such anxiety

Like the worms are already eating me.

So with this sword I pierce my own skin

To make sure I'm alive within.

To see the crimson pour from my flesh

Always was my favorite test.

So I keep on running from all that screams-

I can't escape even in my dreams.

So what am I to do with myself?

Nothing at all! Sweet, Jesus, I need help.

And when he had
given thanks, he
brake it, and said,
Take, eat: this is
my body, which is
broken for you: this
do in remembrance of
me.   1Cr 11:24 KJV

A Broken Man Cannot Be Sold Until He Is Fixed

A faceless flood favors forbidden fruits.

A tasteless touch terrorizes trembling troops.

This army of me has deceived all ecstasy

And I can't see for the debris in the sea.

A nighttime Knight never knows where his sword is.

A lady, lovely and bright, cannot shine in the pit.

Where am I today?

Where are you today?

Can life truly go on this way?

An overflowing objective that is obviously obtuse-

Where is truth today?

Why must these words delay?

Like a forgotten birthday absent of all love

This physicality, a tangible me, is who I like to shove.

So raise up your glasses

And drink a dream to the masses!

So raise up your glasses and wish all this passes!

And like a child crying for his drunken mother, I cannot be bothered.

So I continue cautiously, calloused in the memory of her.

Ah, my Sweet Serenity, so seductive!

Yes, my Passionate Partner, so obstructive!

You grabbed my garment when I did not notice.

I suppose you wanted me to save you.

And one day you will quote this

Because the taste of me will forever stain your lips!

The Voice of a Distant Star Is Still Distant- Even If It Is a Star

The moon is in anguish as she looks down upon her revelers.

A soul, silent and still, stands separated by its own actions of solitude.

He mixes tears with his own blood spilt, sensuously as sorrow fills his heart.

Arms drip crimson droplets like the cherubim's tears, chronicled over history.

He set his aim to be true.

He sent his heart, too, and it grew.

He only had to misconstrue

The words of a lady he never knew.

So his thoughts rapidly, rabidly resound relentlessly

Within his twisted heart; outside he falls apart.

Truly, why would any earthly being love a creature so wicked?

Why would a woman give to him his wishes?

Let the blood pool at his knees as he begs his Master.

He remembers what it's like to give love yet not receive.

The Master acknowledges his servant's sorrows

Yet allows all the stench of rejection to permeate.

The man crawls on the jagged road he paved like a dog returning to its vomit,

Like a man returning to breathing in all that is violent.

He set his aim to be true.

He sent his heart, too, and it grew.

He only had to misconstrue

The words of a lady he never knew.

And why call ye me,
Lord, Lord, and do
not the things which
I say? Luk 6:46 KJV

Worldly Wisdom Will Not Win When We Weep

Nails of Nietzsche hammer His hands!

Diagnosis of Derrida drills its demands!

Freudian fallacy feeds fatuous fantasy.

Camus' clamor creates a classy calamity.

What does not kill you makes you stronger.

Does it allow us to cope a tad longer?

With a widow's weeping we warrant weakness.

To this day I cannot comprehend what this will teach us!

To survive as if animals lusting lowly for leverage,

Air, food, water, and sex are our essential survival beverages.

Are we biological machines bent on a bohemian existence?

Or is it something else, a longing for more than mere circumstance?

Are you content?

Am I to ferment?

In a feverish fervor that favors forgiveness He spoke.

I discard any deviation such as we are a cosmic joke.

So poke around and choke on the sound

As together we break new ground for all around,

Around the globe, breaking through to even the claustrophobe.

Hear me hiss, all of this, as if it were a list!

Help me resist all of this, as if it were death's kiss!

Ah, the golden noise of a newly crowned king:

A visualization that cannot be deceived.

Yes, this wicked existence that weakens out persistence!

To all be put away, one day, by true resistance!

My Beautiful Torment

You will be missed as you walk through my mind
Like a covenant created yet never signed.
Like the star-light that falls into my eyes,
Your golden hair will remind me of the sunrise.

Can I escape erratic elements that you elevate in me?
Can I ascertain an appropriate ambivalence around you?
Can I extend my emotions so that I may be free?
Can I end all this engulfing energy that feels so true?

Why must I travel alone, crawling on this path of glass?
You said you would never leave, and now you scorn my past!
A song you sing sweeter than the Sirens.
My heart beats with my own world's rotations.

Can I break a bond that was of benevolent beginnings?
Can I destroy a disenchanted destiny, so
Disconsolate and discontent?
Can I make merrily a mask that is falsely mending?
Can I try to cavort this by throwing in more torment?

Ah, to be tremendously tormented by life itself would propel my mind
to think for itself!
Yes, a devastation, a distraction would certainly do,
But, alas, it would be back on her and the nothing I can accrue.
I suppose I am just the lapsed lap dog that was so lascivious.
In my head I always thought I was a sensible soul- so chivalrous!

The words fail to explain my brain.
These frail words cannot placate my pain.
I will continue to long for your silky touch
but I must be rid of this tedious torment!
Nevertheless, I know this much:
You are still a love and this pen cannot extinguish your torch,
Yes, you are still a love that will seemingly forever scorch.

Angel of Repetition

I lay my angel inside the tomb I built.
Her eyes once glowed like the blue sky.
It is for this angel all my lives I have spilt,
Yet every time I love anew- another lie, another lie.

Yes, her eyes once glowed like the blue sky
With a luscious life that was the envy of demons.
Yet every time I love anew -another lie, another lie.
A catharsis has set in, void of all feelings,

With a luscious life that was the envy of demons.
And with each word as gentle as the rolling waves of the ocean deep,
A catharsis has set in void of all feelings.
Fly away, dear angel, for I do not deserve a sun- like radiance to keep.

And with each word as gentle as the rolling waves of the ocean deep,
I pierce my heart on this dark church spire for all to hear my cry.
Fly away, dear angel, for I do not deserve a sun- like radiance to keep,
Yet every time I love anew- another lie, another lie.

Yes, I pierce my heart on this dark church spire for all to hear my cry.
Yet every time I love anew- another lie, another lie.
It is for this angel I have burned alive and the blood would be spilt,
And every time I love, I lay my angel inside the tomb I built.

What Was That on TV?

What was that on TV?

A purple shade of homosexuality?

What was that on TV?

Some more fabricated brutality!

We must protect what we must see

Or we shall become demons of anarchy.

Censor the masses to bring them up properly.

Create contrived confusion of Christianity.

Wars!

Hunger!

Constant plunder!

How much longer must we blunder?

Blacken our eyes even if the truth is bloody cries.

Our marching men fight to defend; they still die.

People pursuing prosperity, but stay the pauper.

This is our commission.

Children cry constantly causing cataclysmic chaos.

Yet we need another guitar to save us.

What was that on TV?

Liberals and Conservatives romanticize the people.

What was that on TV?

The news makes us bow down in their cathedral.

The truth should frighten us more than MTV!

All this nonsense is not Christianity.

O wretched man that I
am! Who shall
deliver me from the
body of this death?

Rom 7:24 KJV

Synopsis

My being burns with hatred of life.

Why the world survives I'll never know.

So I jump in line and hack at my wrist with a knife.

I am so consumed with sadness I don't see the winter for the snow.

Love in a world of hate is an ironic statement.

Where's my mother? She's out getting wasted!

So my excuses are real, raw and uncut:

I can sin because of what was within!

My life was rough, so I will drink until I vomit!

Consume the sin! You know you love it!

Yet all this nonsense rots me like sun- dried wood.

The flies have laid their maggots and I decay.

Screams of pain are echoed back by demons,

Taunting me and disillusioning me with hopes,

Distorting my eyes and controlling my life.

Death is the door and these pills are the key;

With a tear filled pillow this is how I'll be free.

The cold tendrils of his sweet embrace entice me,

The lullaby of his voice is too lovely to be evil.

So I replay these moments in real time.

I continue to enjoy my life and die some.

 Die some.

There is no cure for myself.

There is no cure for myself.

Where are You? Is this dead feeling You?

I yell at night to feel something. God, please let me feel You!

All I get is vacancy, emptiness and my ultimate loneliness.

I am so insignificant; I do not deserve to garner Your attention.

I am so hate- consumed; I don't deserve my own mother's affection!

So who am I to question Your ways?

If You are absent, there must be a reason.

One day I will hear Your voice;

One day I will give You my choice.

The walls are broken and all I have to show are bloody knuckles

Your words I have never heard, yet are familiar.

This can't be real, but this pain I feel- now that's real!

God- like nonsense is for the weak and ignorant.

Wait, that's me! I'm almost dead.

I don't want to be happy with the night.

I no longer wish to spit at Your light.

As I cry out, I give you myself.

Take me away from me; this life is dead.

I want to die in You; now I cry in You!

It's all over.

Now I begin.

With God on my side, whom can I offend?

I acknowledge I am still a weak and wretched creature!

I will no longer cry alone when the world kills.

I now have Him, even if I still need these pills.

He took it all away, my hate and my blood,

Lord, only You can calm the rising flood.

Ian Rant

Well, the past few days have been pointless and numb. I suppose I did that to myself. Is this fun? This empty feeling of being out all night laughing and spewing forth quips so all may laugh? Is chain smoking fun? Is drinking supposed to be fun? It's all empty. It's all meaningless. I hate it all!!! I am about to fall off and I know it. I can feel it happening. Some doubts slithered in my head last night about God . . . While I was driving in a Jeep with the top off, I stared at the night sky just asking questions in my head . . . . I am not proud of my doubts at all . . . but I keep falling and falling. I can visualize the actual decent into oblivion. I see myself, limbs flailing wildly in the air, just plunging further and further into the recess of a hell I have created, an abyss of my own inner self. Well let's see how much further I fall tonight. Please, God, save me from myself.

Falling, Falling

Cracked and fissured like a thirsty man's lifeless lips.

Crumbled and fragmented like a teenage love letter.

Cancerous and voracious, my love for life rips,

Rips into a ravishing reborn royal,

Rips into my skin as I work and toil.

The relentless ripping is the result of one who rebelled, to be exalted above the congregation.

It was a wondrous yet wistful display of heavenly bodies, falling, falling.

Bet WE are heavenly bodies.

We are also the evil one's favorite hobby!

Tempting Tempter of ages past,

Falling, falling with him into that pitiful pit.

Tormenting Torturer, your miserable myth overcomes us so fast.

Falling, falling into the outer darkness we agree to worship.

O, Lucifer, son of the morning! [how] art thou cut down to the ground,

You who didst weaken the nations!

Inviting and intruding, you open your empty- grave smile all over creation!

The only relief from one of such might is from a suffering God-man on a crucifix!

The only possible power we have to parry your persistent tricks!

O Lucifer, like a cherished only child, you were once so loved!

But the death of the Messiah was for us and not the heavenly not above.

You keep falling, falling. I pity a being that was so esteemed and once so high.

But you keep falling, falling, like a burden laden animal with each and every try.

With each and every sigh and cry that was the result in every lie

The closer we draw nigh, the closer we become to the Most High!

Where Am I Headed?

For instance, isn't it lovely to be held prisoner by one's own mind?
I am a recluse and what I long for, I cannot find.
If I could put my hand across my own throat,
If I would be so kind, I would do it in the mirror to watch me choke,
Choke on the debris that is a society without a key,
Without a clue all wound up in acidic glue!
This tapestry of my life explains the burn marks on my flesh.
This crying boy in me is as profane as the patrons of this bar.
Red, white, black and blue is the American way!
What am I to accrue if I cannot control my urges for life?
A life, deadly as the sharpest knife!
I cannot sleep for the torture is too deep,
As deep as a suicidal leap off a bridge.

It cannot be this way!
It cannot be this way!

Alas it is, a way I have fallen a slave to,
Slave to all this world has to offer.
Yes, it offers it up like a religious man opening up his coffers,
To pour the scrapes and bruises of a work's day
All to feel alive- all to feel depraved.

Nighttime Angel

Silent garden, sweet life, overtake the night with violent strife!
Bruised soul of paradise, unfound, lonely and profound without my
sound,
Lost, you were lovely once like invisible whispers overcome by dusk.

Turn me over I cannot see!
Turn me over I cannot be!

Trapped in a net meant for stars' potential
Never met like empty broken jars.
Are we all the same children, cold and unloved,
In a creamy tar existence that is too far,
Far from what our heads can comprehend?
Do we pretend and let our smiles defend
The onslaught of this world?
Curled in balls of fury and sadness crying into a mess
And creating a salty sea of insanity.
Far be it from me to say that I am okay or that today
Is the day, when all I see is constant decay!
No, it's better for me to suffer under the burden,
For I'd rather do that than placate.
My grin is not here for me, but for you,
As is my sin, so that all the world can see all that is untrue,
As untrue as a word unspoken to keep a man's ego wide:
As untrue as a broken heart that continues to love a lie

After the same manner
also he took the
cup, when he had
supped, saying, This
cup is the new
testament in my
blood: this do ye, as
oft as ye drink it ,
in remembrance of me.

1 Cr 11:25 KJV

Ironic Salvation

Oh what a twisted man I must be

When darkness makes me feel free!

I love to stumble around with arms out stretched -

I am happy to admit that these wounds make me feel refreshed.

The nicotine of my soul is my belief in inebriation-

Altered states and nights of feminine embraces!

Yeah, this is how I inflict myself on others.

I am proud they think I am a waste.

I hate the sun it makes me feel dirty.

The penetrating rays feel like the eyes of God are on me.

It tries to expose and burn out the evil.

This is why I sleep all day and live in my dreams.

This is true freedom and I have no need for constraints.

That is all we are, a multitude of rules and laws acting out!

Wait! Turn that mirror around!

I gasp at what I see. Those people I criticized are better off than me!

I believed I was free when I was trapped in my misery!

They used to say I was a slave to sin; I'd smirk and say they were a
slave to Him!

But I am! I am entranced and hypnotized by evil's perfume- like scent.

I cannot break these chains I placed on myself.

This revelation that He is real- it cannot be!

I cannot stare at my own reflection, it must be!

So I cry out on my knees,

Lord, God, *please save me*!

Level 9

Bound in brilliant illusions are my wrists,
Captured and frozen like water granules in a mist,
And they persist to insist like a growing cyst.

I demand a detoxification of this man!

The lies surround me like a horde of savages,
Waiting to march on me in a mere moment.
I try to stare at the sun but my eyes are ravaged.
God's gallant graces growing, so I never stop to gallivant.

Look up!
Look down!
Shut up!
Sit down!

Cast aside that pride- manufactured crown!
Stand astride with nose to the ground!
Can you hear Satan's teeth enjoying your defeat?
In your mind you won- this is deceit-
For in fact the Inferno groans for your bones.
The torturing tongues of flames are already consuming you.
My Judas, truly I wish you'd stop what you do.
But I suppose the silver of greed is better than the gold of me.
Yes, my Judas, betrayer of betrayers, false hope conceived,
With each twist of the knife you fall further.
With each droplet of blood you raise up a black empire.
Spin the blade tearing tissue as the red now forms at my lips.
Save the parade saying I miss you as the blue sky fades from your finger tips.
And when your throne is gone, do not ask for my help,
For when you sat in it (when it was mine), you just watched me yelp.

How cruel can a friend be in his own fantasy!
This question is answered when a feminine embrace is more important than all you see.

Random Ian Quote:

Where has this wisdom sprung? With a wink of an eye it all comes undone. For is it better to love than never to have at all, but I say is it better to be stabbed to a crimson mess than never at all?

Everyday is Wednesday

Make sense of this. Make sense of me means
I am not within the means of what man marvels.
To what wayward beast do they raise up their sacrifices of
Sweat, blood and tears, allowing sorrows to be taken by fears and
beers?

And Wednesday is everyday when the years lose track of themselves,
And Wednesday is everyday when we only hear the words outside
ourselves.

I do not want to drown dreadfully and bleed bleakly in the images of
humanity.
Without this mark of approval I cannot buy nor trade.
Without this heart of evil these mortal messages will begin to fade.
I am a chaotic clone contrived from collected cultures.
I am a label within a label within a label within a fabricated fable's
fracture
Of the brokenness of our bodies. We need the Brokenness of His
body.

And Wednesday is everyday when the years lose track of themselves,
And Wednesday is everyday when we only hear the words outside
ourselves.

Pieces of peppermint turn into piles of pollution.
Good intentions never met cannot be the solution!
You cannot clean a dirty bowl just externally;
It must be cleansed from within, just as our sin, eternally.
Can you force a tree not to be a tree?
Can you force me not to be me?
You can call a tree anything your meandering mind wishes it to be
But, in truth, the tree is a tree and I am me.

And Wednesday is everyday when the years lose track of themselves,
And Wednesday is everyday when we only hear the words outside
ourselves.

Listen to what I say!
Listen to what I say!

Believe me or not, this is in fact reality.
Not some distorted demonic man- made fallacy,
One that speaks sweet cyanide into our lives,
Or one that gently lulls us into death's eyes.
Do not lean unto your own understanding!
This all seems to be the evil one's philandering,
To mock us as the ages roll about,
To trap us in a devastating darkness as we scrape our skin and shout!

And Wednesday is everyday when the years lose track of themselves
And Wednesday is everyday when we only hear the words outside
ourselves,
And Wednesday is everyday when society forces distortion into our
heads,
And Wednesday is everyday when we create
a cohesion that, upon being inhaled,
we become dead!

For that which I do I
allow not: for what I
would, that do I not;
but what I hate, that
do I. Rom 7:15 KJV

Can We Do Good?

What a contrived confusion I have become!

Like a bird with no wings I am useless.

My soul is a bear, bellowing for beauty.

My heart is a porous parasite that preys on acidity.

The burning blackness of my bones hastens my demise.

Why must I open my eyes to see the sun rise?

The day to me is a fallen angel's prison

Wearily wrapped up with all the world's wisdom.

Ah, thinkers of the world unite!

Yes, fix us, make things right!

We cannot trust ourselves how can we follow you?

All we do is lust after ourselves and become crueler.

I expect elaborate ends to everything in existence,

For it is all evil, blanketed in human persistence.

Ah, to do nothing would be the solution!

Yes, to do nothing would cease the spiritual pollution,

The pollution that poisons the most prepared person!

You cannot plan for perfection to produce sin.

Why must it be the weakest mind full of anxiety?

The one that writes so elaborately, the one you now see?

Create me and break me: it's the only way I can live.

Masticate me and rape me: it's the path I pretend upon,

A proud pauper possessing only his thoughts.

Oh, this is all this world is a construct of

Our impulses initiated into actions,

Impulses that have no eternal satisfaction!

Let us do nothing, then, for all we do is evil!

Even the good we garner is gratification of self.

Our selfish insecurities drive us to sanity,

A sanity full of insanity!

A normality full of abnormalities!

What is wickedness if we define our own existence?

Who is able to rise and rebel for resistance?

Let us be lemming -like lessons for future ages,

Reproducing intelligence and banishing it to cages.

What is standard?

What is average?

What is right?

What is wrong?

Do I have the knowledge of God to decipher such things?

None of us do, we are all evil beings.

Again I say, "Do nothing" for all we do is create guilt.

Yes, do nothing, for it's our fault God's blood was spilt!

Save the Slave

What are we fighting for?
Struggling to adore
A make-up caked whore?
What are we striving for?
Increase profits to acquire more-
Decrease ourselves and become poor?
What are we trying for?
Genuflecting knees are sore
And talking to God is a chore.
What are we dying for?
The chance to finally ignore
A reunion to restore.

Restore yourself.
Restore me.

Lord, what are we fighting for?
Beautiful lies engaging the whore.
Babylon! You entice my soul!
Babylon! Breaking my brain,
Gunmetal pain etched by acid rain.
I hallucinate reality when, clearly,
My God is what is changing me.

Oh, Lord, design and define me.
Oh, Lord, refine me one more time!
What is wrong with my actions?
Satisfaction of emptiness engulfs reactions!
Is this how I exist?
How do I resist
The red lipstick kiss,
The whore's lips,
Babylon's tricks!

Oh, ABBA, save me from this!

The Question

Quickening my awakening upon which I ask a question,

Would the blood leak gentler if I only used a pin?

Would lavish, luminous lives look back upon my serendipitous sin?

Would lies and lies and what lies in me be my lesson?

Would I have to retrace this ragged repetition?

Like a ceaseless fluttering of leaves within a wind's rotation,

Yes, like a resounding, relentless, rigid, remorseful rotation,

These answers I must find-but first, my question-

I must repeat my previous, uneventful repetition:

But truly, would the suffering be eased if struck with a pin?

And why must I languish in anguish from such a lesson?

For when the blood bellows brushing my toes, how can I *not* sin?

It is my understanding that we are all in sin,

A never-ending, abysmal, dismal and pitiful rotation.

My penance is suffering and my suffering my penance lesson.

Therefore, my delightful death to self and achievement is an ironic question.

How can I deceive my extended finger with this pin

As I continue to pride fully prick it in constant repetition?

And it is my decision to proceed in this repetition.

And it is my conclusion to proceed in this sin,

As I wonder if my faltering finger will ever become calloused by this pin,

Jabbing, jamming, stabbing and slamming in this ruthless rotation.

Still I continue circularly clamoring with this question:

Is suffering the *only* way to show us our lesson?

Are we so flattering to ourselves that our propriety is our lesson-
One where we are eventually punished in our ongoing repetition?
Again, there is that lingering, lasting question:
If we are in sin, and constantly continue to sin,
Over and over and over again, in a broken rotation,
Broken like a layer of skin, slowly pricked by a pin,

Wherein the blood colors the gray as my skin holds the pin,
What is released? The life within. It is a painful lesson.
It is an endless process, enduring upon our death's final rotation.
It is a thankless progress wherein we wish no repetition.
Yet it is too bad, for we are all in sin.
So it would seem I have answered my own question.

There is a reason for this pin within our repetition
And the lesson is that without suffering we know not of sin.
My own thoughts' rotation has finally ended with this: was that even
the question?

```
From Galatia to You.
Welcome to ME.
```

```
You can see what big
letters I make when I
write with my own hand!
```

A vacation becomes disastrous and deadly if you do not return.

Smiles of liquid pool on our chins, ready to be frozen if life becomes cold.

We are afraid to show you who we are!

But God sees our plastic parade of pornography,

Perpetual placation of self flattery.

Salamander, amphibious, double-edged and broken we stand!

```
You can see what big
letters I make when I
write with my own hand!
```

Twinkle your eyes for stars that rise do so as well.

They also twinkle when they tumble to Hell!

 Dwell upon all I say for truth lies under our tongue.

It rebels when confronted and thus becomes numb.

Poppy seed excuses will not work when at judgment we stand . . .

You can see what big
letters I make when I
write with my own hand!

His Cry

He penetrates purposely, protruding and prepared.
We are only mutts of hell, and not pure-bred.
We cry and complain only never to attain
What we can truly be called and leave this pain,
A paradoxical parry that prepares us for our peril.
We can only find happiness in death upon our burial.
Our evil envisions external joy.
How can a being be so coy?

To be content is all we can lament.

Now let us tilt our head to the sky.
Now let us recognize why He died.
Now let us tilt our head to the sky
And taste the salinity as God cries.

Wars and rumors of war are all we are.
Self imposed constant joy is a star way too far.
Our mouths ajar yet full of decaying tar.
Our prayers are pretend and can never be for you.
I say these so we do not misconstrue.
Black are our hearts since the very start.
And ever since, we continue to fall apart.
We drown our sorrows in women and wine
And our tongues twist our words serpentine.

To be content is all we can lament.

Now let us tilt our head to the sky.
Now let us recognize why He died.
Now let us tilt our head to the sky
And taste the salinity as God cries.

<u>His Cry</u>   11/12/05

1   He penatrates purposley protecting + prepared
2   We are only mats of hell + not punished
3   We cry + complain only never to attain
4   What we can truly be called + leave this pain
5   A paradoxal parry that prepares for our peril
6   We can only find happiness in death + pon our burial
7   Our evil envisions eternal joy
8   How could a being be so coy?
9   To be content is all we can lament
    Now let us tilt our head to the sky
    Now let us recognize why he died
    Now let us tilt our head to the sky
    And taste the salinity as God cries

1   Wars + rumors of wars are all we are
2   Self imposed constant joy is a star way too far
3   Our mouths ajar yet full of decaying tar
4   Our prayers we pretend + can never be for You
5   I say these so we do not misconstrue
6   Black is our heart since the very start
7   And ever since we continue to fall apart
8   We drown our senses in women + wine
9   And our tongues twist our words serpentine
    Now let us tilt our head to the sky
    Now let us recognize why he died
    Now let us tilt our head to the sky
    And taste the salinity as God cries

60

Jesus saith unto him, I am the way, the truth, and the life: no man cometh unto the Father, but by me. Jhn 14:6 KJV

Pound

I look luminously into life's liquid levitation
I bend my face with a possessed hesitation . . .

Pound! Pound! Pound! Holding on to the insides, so it may not leap
out and dry!
The footsteps of the daily man pound, pound, pound into my being.
The church bells pound, pound, and pound to bring in those fleeing.

Pound! Pound! Pound! The cross is quickly lifted into place
As you have no choice but to spread disjointed arms!

I have broken my body like dirty shattered glass punched through
I have taken frustrating sexual ecstasy to replace this broken fool.

Pound! Pound! Pound! Why have you forsaken me?
Pound! Pound! Pound! The clinging and clanging continue to tear
apart!
Clinging and clanging, pounding and pulsating,
The ringing of the hammer, the gnashing of teeth,
The moaning of souls selected for judgment,
The groaning of souls selected for punishment.

Pound! Pound! Pound! Is the sound of the sin all around!
Pound! Pound! Pound! Is the sound of Him bleeding His crown!
The tint of crimson can be seen from afar as they pound, pound,
pound!

The clinging and clacking, the cracking and smacking,
All as the hammer pounds, Pounds, POUNDS!

Benevolent blood broken by the swinging of the sound of the hammer
that Pounds! Pounds! Pounds!

All for an emotional enigma, an erratic figure
All for the broken bystander who was clinging
To the clanging of the swaying hammer,
Pounding!

Pounding into His Holy flesh for forgiveness.
Pound! Pound! Pound!
I do not deserve this.

Hello

Crucifixus est dei filius; non pudet, quia pudendum est.
Et mortuus est dei filius; credibile prorsus est, quia ineptum est.
Et sepultus resurrexit; certum est, quia impossibile.

De Carne Christi (*The Flesh of Christ*)
Tertullian, 155-230 AD.

Languishing Language
Anguishing Appendage!
Bloody Beacon
Deceived Deacon!

Buy me
Buy the

Annotated Autobiography!

Shapeless Seas
Silent Storms!
Shapely Sleaze
Pious Porn!

That's me-
Ghosts of sorrows,
Sabbath left unholy,
Most arrows
Miss completely.

(A man's absurd paradoxical plan to be heard)

Hello, my name is Nothing Clean.
I am worth tripe in the eyes of you.
I was almost dead on the streets of your world.
I almost succumbed to the lovely taste of the depraved.

        Oh, and did I mention alcohol.
Oh, and did I mention sex.
        Oh, and did I mention alcohol.
Oh, and did I mention depressed.

Hello, I am still here, Attention- sex- fiend.
I can scream more than you!
I was almost captivated by this world.
I almost fell victim to the sin parade.

Oh, and did I mention self mutilation.
Oh, and did I mention depressed.
Oh, and did I mention self mutilation.
Oh, and did I mention divorced mess.

Hello, my mommy and daddy left when I was 15.
I can cry more than you.
I was almost married in this world.
I almost didn't realize Eros and being enslaved.

Oh, and did I mention pill popping.
Oh, and did I mention divorced mess.
Oh, and did I mention pill popping.
Oh, and did I mention death's bridal dress.

Hello, I like drinking and drugs-
I can do more than you!
I was almost drugged by this world.
I almost walked in the shadows of the afraid.

Oh, and did you think I was going to mention something.
Oh, and did you think I was going to mention death's bridal dress.
Oh, and did you think I was going to mention something.
Oh, and did you think was going to mention success.

(The end to a man's absurd paradoxical plan to be heard)

Language is leveled.
Language is mine.
Language is longing.
Language of my time!

Speak! Speak!
Pharisees condemn Christ.
Religious happy- flowery –dancing-
Smiley- factory- manufactured by humanity. . .

Crucify Him! Crucify Him!
Slamming shouts in my face.
Fists fruitfully fall even though clean from sin.
Nails narrate the narrative of my case.

Sew my speech -so I may be silent.
Sew my preach- even though it's violent.
Sow what you reap- your harvest is done.
Sow as you reap- God loads His gun.

      HE HAS COME!
      HE HAS COME!

With a tongue-like sword He has won.
I no longer must suffer.

      HE HAS COME!
      IT IS DONE!

And without controversy great is the mystery of godliness: God was manifest in the flesh, justified in the Spirit, seen of angels, preached unto the Gentiles, believed on in the world, received up into glory.

1Ti 3:16 KJV